Copyright © 2023 by B. R. Breathing (Author)

All rights reserved. No part of this book may be reproduced or utilized in any form or by any means, electronic or mechanical, including photocopying, recording or by any information storage and retrieval system, without permission in writing from the publisher, except for brief quotations in critical articles or reviews.

The content of this book is based on various sources and is intended for educational and entertainment purposes only. While the author has made every effort to ensure the accuracy, completeness, and reliability of the information provided, the information may be subject to errors, omissions, or inaccuracies. Therefore, the author makes no warranties, express or implied, regarding the content of this book.

Readers are advised to seek the guidance of a licensed professional before attempting any techniques or actions outlined in this book. The author is not responsible for any losses, damages, or injuries that may arise from the use of information contained within. The information provided in this book is not intended to be a substitute for professional advice, and readers should not rely solely on the information presented.

By reading this book, readers acknowledge that the author is not providing legal, financial, medical, or professional advice. Any reliance on the information contained in this book is solely at the reader's own risk.

Thank you for selecting this book as a valuable source of knowledge and inspiration. Our aim is to provide you with insights and information that will enrich your understanding and enhance your personal growth. We appreciate your decision to embark on this journey of discovery with us, and we hope that this book will exceed your expectations and leave a lasting impact on your life.

Title: Mindfulness for Beginners: Discovering Inner Peace and Happiness

Subtitle: A Step-by-Step Guide to Cultivating Mindfulness in Daily Life

Series: The Mindful Life Series: Cultivating Awareness and Connection in Everyday Living

Author: B. R. Breathing

Table of Contents

Introduction **6**
   What is mindfulness?..6
   What is meditation?.. 10
   Why are mindfulness and meditation important for mental and emotional well-being? 12

Chapter 1: Mindfulness **14**
   What is mindfulness and how does it differ from meditation? 14
   The benefits of mindfulness for mental and emotional well-being..17
   The science behind mindfulness: how it affects the brain and body...20
   Techniques for practicing mindfulness in daily life 23

Chapter 2: Meditation.. **26**
   What is meditation and how does it differ from mindfulness? 26
   The benefits of meditation for mental and emotional well-being 29
   The science behind meditation: how it affects the brain and body...32
   Techniques for practicing meditation, including breath awareness, body scan, and loving-kindness meditation 34

Chapter 3: Establishing a Meditation Practice **37**

Setting up a meditation space *37*
Finding the right time of day to meditate *40*
Developing a regular meditation practice *43*
Overcoming common challenges in meditation *46*

Chapter 4: Mindfulness-Based Stress Reduction .. 50
The connection between stress and mental health *50*
How mindfulness can reduce stress *53*
Techniques for using mindfulness to manage stress in daily life *56*
Mindful breathing exercises and body scans *59*

Chapter 5: Mindfulness and Relationships 62
How mindfulness can improve relationships *62*
Mindful communication *66*
Active listening *69*
Developing empathy and compassion *71*

Chapter 6: Mindfulness and Productivity 76
How mindfulness can improve productivity *76*
Techniques for practicing mindfulness in the workplace 78
Overcoming distractions and staying focused *81*
Using mindfulness to prioritize tasks *83*

Chapter 7: Mindfulness and Self-Compassion 85
How mindfulness can help develop self-compassion *85*
Practicing self-compassion in daily life *87*
Overcoming self-criticism *90*

Cultivating a sense of gratitude and appreciation 92
Conclusion **95**
The benefits of mindfulness and meditation for mental and emotional well-being 95
Encouragement to continue practicing mindfulness and meditation 98
Further resources for exploring mindfulness and meditation 101
Wordbook **103**
Supplementary Materials **105**

Introduction
What is mindfulness?

In today's fast-paced world, it's easy to get caught up in the constant flow of information and distractions. Mindfulness offers a way to slow down and become more present in the moment, allowing us to experience life fully and reduce stress and anxiety. This chapter will provide an in-depth exploration of the concept of mindfulness, including its definition, history, and benefits.

What is Mindfulness?

Mindfulness is the practice of paying attention to the present moment, without judgment. It involves intentionally bringing awareness to our thoughts, feelings, and sensations, with a sense of openness and curiosity. Mindfulness has its roots in ancient Buddhist traditions but has been adapted for secular use in modern psychology and mental health treatment.

The concept of mindfulness can be traced back to the teachings of the Buddha over 2,500 years ago. The Buddha taught that mindfulness was a path to liberation from suffering and a means of achieving enlightenment. Mindfulness was originally practiced as part of Buddhist meditation, and over time, it became a central aspect of Buddhist philosophy.

In the 20th century, mindfulness began to gain popularity in the West, thanks to the work of pioneers such as Jon Kabat-Zinn. Kabat-Zinn developed a mindfulness-based stress reduction program that brought mindfulness into the mainstream of Western medicine and psychology. Since then, mindfulness has been used in a variety of settings, including healthcare, education, and the workplace.

The Benefits of Mindfulness:

Research has shown that mindfulness can have a wide range of benefits for mental and physical health. Some of the benefits of mindfulness include:

1. Stress Reduction: Mindfulness can help reduce stress by reducing the activation of the body's stress response system. By bringing awareness to the present moment, mindfulness can help us let go of worries and anxieties about the past and the future.

2. Improved Emotional Regulation: Mindfulness can help us regulate our emotions by increasing our awareness of them. When we become more aware of our emotions, we are better able to regulate them and respond to them in a healthy way.

3. Enhanced Cognitive Function: Mindfulness has been shown to improve cognitive function, including attention, memory, and decision-making.

4. Increased Resilience: Mindfulness can increase resilience to stress and adversity by helping us develop a sense of inner strength and stability.

5. Improved Relationships: Mindfulness can improve our relationships by helping us become more present and attentive to others, increasing empathy and compassion.

6. Physical Health: Mindfulness has been shown to have a positive impact on physical health, including reducing blood pressure and improving immune function.

Techniques for Practicing Mindfulness:

There are many different techniques for practicing mindfulness, including:

1. Mindful Breathing: Focusing on the breath is a simple and effective way to bring attention to the present moment.

2. Body Scan: A body scan involves bringing awareness to each part of the body, one at a time.

3. Mindful Movement: Mindful movement involves bringing awareness to the body's movements, such as during yoga or walking.

4. Mindful Eating: Mindful eating involves paying close attention to the senses during the act of eating, such as the taste, texture, and smell of the food.

Conclusion:

Mindfulness is a powerful tool for improving mental and physical health, and it can be practiced in many different ways. By cultivating mindfulness in our lives, we can experience greater clarity, calm, and well-being. In the next chapter, we will explore the concept of meditation and how it differs from mindfulness.

What is meditation?

Meditation is a practice that involves training the mind to focus on the present moment, often through a combination of breathing techniques and visualization exercises. While meditation has been practiced for thousands of years in various cultures, it has gained significant popularity in recent years as a way to improve mental and emotional well-being.

At its core, meditation involves cultivating a state of heightened awareness and attention, allowing individuals to better understand their own thoughts and emotions. Rather than being swept up in the stresses and distractions of everyday life, meditation helps individuals develop a sense of inner peace and stillness, allowing them to better manage their emotions and reactions.

While there are many different forms of meditation, most involve some form of concentration or visualization technique. One of the most common types of meditation is breath awareness, which involves focusing on the sensation of breathing and using it as an anchor for the mind. Other techniques include body scan meditations, which involve slowly scanning the body and bringing awareness to each part, and loving-kindness meditations, which involve focusing on feelings of compassion and kindness towards oneself and others.

In addition to promoting mental and emotional well-being, research has shown that meditation can have a number of physical health benefits as well. For example, regular meditation practice has been linked to reduced inflammation, improved immune function, and lower blood pressure.

Despite its many benefits, meditation can be challenging to incorporate into one's daily routine. Developing a consistent practice requires discipline and commitment, and it can take time to build up the skills necessary to fully reap the benefits of meditation. However, with patience and dedication, anyone can learn to meditate and experience the profound effects it can have on their life.

In the following chapters, we will explore various techniques for practicing meditation, as well as the science behind how it affects the brain and body. We will also discuss tips for establishing a regular meditation practice, including setting up a meditation space and finding the right time of day to meditate.

Why are mindfulness and meditation important for mental and emotional well-being?

Mindfulness and meditation are practices that have been shown to have a significant impact on mental and emotional well-being. In today's fast-paced world, many individuals struggle with stress, anxiety, and other mental health issues, and mindfulness and meditation offer a way to manage these challenges and cultivate greater emotional resilience.

One of the primary benefits of mindfulness and meditation is their ability to help individuals develop greater awareness and control over their thoughts and emotions. By learning to observe one's thoughts and feelings without judgment, individuals can better manage negative emotions like anxiety and depression and cultivate a greater sense of inner peace and calm.

In addition to reducing negative emotions, mindfulness and meditation have also been shown to improve positive emotions like happiness and contentment. By focusing on the present moment and cultivating gratitude and appreciation for what one has, individuals can develop a greater sense of satisfaction and fulfillment in life.

Another important benefit of mindfulness and meditation is their ability to improve cognitive functioning.

Research has shown that these practices can enhance attention, memory, and decision-making, making it easier to stay focused and productive throughout the day.

Perhaps most importantly, mindfulness and meditation have been shown to have a significant impact on stress reduction. Chronic stress has been linked to a wide range of negative health outcomes, from cardiovascular disease to depression, and mindfulness and meditation have been shown to be effective in managing stress and reducing its impact on the body and mind.

Overall, mindfulness and meditation are important tools for promoting mental and emotional well-being. By learning to cultivate greater awareness and control over one's thoughts and emotions, individuals can better manage stress, reduce negative emotions, and cultivate greater happiness and fulfillment in life. In the following chapters, we will explore the science behind mindfulness and meditation, as well as practical tips for incorporating these practices into your daily routine.

Chapter 1: Mindfulness
What is mindfulness and how does it differ from meditation?

Mindfulness is the practice of bringing one's attention to the present moment and observing one's thoughts and feelings without judgment. It involves developing a greater awareness of one's inner experience, including thoughts, emotions, and physical sensations, and learning to accept these experiences with compassion and curiosity.

Meditation, on the other hand, is a practice that can take many forms but generally involves a deliberate effort to focus the mind on a specific object or idea. This can include practices like breath awareness, body scan, and loving-kindness meditation, among others.

While mindfulness and meditation are often used interchangeably, there are some important differences between the two practices. Mindfulness can be thought of as a way of being in the world, a way of paying attention to one's experiences in a nonjudgmental way. Meditation, on the other hand, is a specific tool or technique that can be used to cultivate mindfulness.

Another key difference between mindfulness and meditation is their focus. Mindfulness is about being present and aware of one's inner experiences in the moment, while meditation is about focusing the mind on a specific object or idea. This can include a physical sensation like the breath, a visual image, or a word or phrase, depending on the type of meditation being practiced.

Another way to think about the difference between mindfulness and meditation is in terms of their goals. Mindfulness is about developing a greater awareness and acceptance of one's experiences in the moment, while meditation is about training the mind to focus and concentrate on a specific object or idea. Both practices can be used to improve mental and emotional well-being, but they approach this goal in different ways.

It's worth noting that mindfulness and meditation are not mutually exclusive practices, and many meditation techniques involve elements of mindfulness. For example, in loving-kindness meditation, practitioners are encouraged to cultivate feelings of kindness and compassion toward themselves and others, which can promote greater mindfulness and awareness of one's inner experience.

In the next section, we will explore the benefits of mindfulness for mental and emotional well-being, including its impact on stress reduction and cognitive functioning. We will also delve into the science behind mindfulness, including how it affects the brain and body, and discuss techniques for practicing mindfulness in daily life.

The benefits of mindfulness for mental and emotional well-being

The practice of mindfulness has been shown to have a number of benefits for mental and emotional well-being. In this section, we'll explore some of the key benefits of mindfulness and how it can improve our overall health and well-being.

1. Reducing Stress and Anxiety One of the most well-known benefits of mindfulness is its ability to reduce stress and anxiety. Research has shown that practicing mindfulness regularly can help to lower levels of cortisol, the stress hormone, in the body. This can lead to a decrease in symptoms of anxiety, depression, and other mental health conditions.

Mindfulness can also help us to become more aware of our thoughts and emotions, allowing us to better manage and regulate our responses to stressors. With regular practice, mindfulness can help us to develop a greater sense of calm and equanimity in the face of difficult situations.

2. Improving Emotional Regulation Another benefit of mindfulness is its ability to improve emotional regulation. By practicing mindfulness, we can become more aware of our emotional states and learn to observe them without judgment. This can help us to respond to our emotions in a

more intentional and adaptive way, rather than reacting impulsively.

Mindfulness can also help us to cultivate positive emotions like gratitude, compassion, and joy. By focusing our attention on positive experiences and emotions, we can train our brains to become more attuned to these experiences and develop a more positive outlook on life.

3. Enhancing Cognitive Functioning In addition to its impact on emotional regulation, mindfulness has been shown to enhance cognitive functioning. Research has demonstrated that regular mindfulness practice can lead to improvements in working memory, attention, and decision-making.

This is because mindfulness helps to strengthen the prefrontal cortex, the part of the brain responsible for executive function and decision-making. By practicing mindfulness, we can improve our ability to focus our attention, regulate our emotions, and make better decisions.

4. Improving Sleep Quality Poor sleep is a common problem that can have a negative impact on mental and emotional well-being. Fortunately, mindfulness has been shown to improve sleep quality by reducing stress and anxiety and promoting relaxation.

Research has found that practicing mindfulness before bed can lead to improvements in sleep quality and duration. By cultivating a greater sense of relaxation and calm, we can improve our ability to fall asleep and stay asleep throughout the night.

5. Enhancing Relationships Finally, mindfulness can also have a positive impact on our relationships with others. By practicing mindfulness, we can become more attuned to our own emotions and better able to regulate our responses to others. This can lead to improved communication, empathy, and compassion in our relationships with others.

In addition, mindfulness can also help us to cultivate a greater sense of gratitude and appreciation for the people in our lives. By focusing our attention on the positive aspects of our relationships, we can strengthen our connections with others and experience greater levels of social support and well-being.

Overall, the benefits of mindfulness for mental and emotional well-being are numerous and far-reaching. By practicing mindfulness regularly, we can improve our overall health and well-being and enhance our ability to navigate the challenges of daily life. In the next section, we'll explore the science behind mindfulness and how it affects the brain and body.

The science behind mindfulness: how it affects the brain and body

The practice of mindfulness has gained significant attention in recent years, not just as a way to reduce stress and anxiety, but also as a way to enhance overall well-being. While mindfulness has been used for centuries in Eastern traditions, modern neuroscience is just beginning to uncover the mechanisms behind its many benefits.

The brain is a complex and constantly evolving organ that is responsible for our thoughts, emotions, and behaviors. Through brain imaging studies, scientists have discovered that mindfulness can have a profound impact on brain structure and function.

One of the key findings is that mindfulness meditation can increase the thickness of the prefrontal cortex, the part of the brain that is responsible for executive functions such as decision making, problem-solving, and emotion regulation. This suggests that regular practice of mindfulness can improve cognitive abilities and emotional regulation.

Studies have also shown that mindfulness can increase activity in the amygdala, the part of the brain that is responsible for the fight-or-flight response. This increased activity may seem counterintuitive, as mindfulness is often associated with relaxation and calmness. However, it is believed that through mindfulness, individuals can learn to observe their thoughts and emotions without judgment, allowing them to respond to stressful situations in a more adaptive and effective manner.

Furthermore, mindfulness has been found to reduce activity in the default mode network, a network of brain regions that is activated when our minds are at rest and not engaged in a task. This network is associated with self-referential thinking, such as worrying about the past or future, and can contribute to symptoms of anxiety and depression. By reducing activity in this network, mindfulness can help individuals become more present-focused and less preoccupied with negative thoughts.

In addition to its effects on the brain, mindfulness can also have physical benefits. Chronic stress is associated with a range of negative health outcomes, such as cardiovascular disease, diabetes, and immune dysfunction. By reducing stress levels, mindfulness can help mitigate the negative effects of chronic stress on the body.

Studies have shown that mindfulness can reduce inflammation, a key contributor to many chronic health conditions. In one study, participants who practiced mindfulness meditation for eight weeks had lower levels of the inflammatory marker C-reactive protein compared to a control group. Mindfulness has also been found to reduce blood pressure, another important risk factor for cardiovascular disease.

Overall, the scientific evidence suggests that mindfulness can have a profound impact on both the brain and body, leading to improvements in cognitive function, emotional regulation, and physical health.

Techniques for practicing mindfulness in daily life

Mindfulness can be practiced in many ways throughout daily life. The following techniques can help you integrate mindfulness into your daily routine:

1. Mindful Breathing: One of the easiest ways to practice mindfulness is through mindful breathing. Simply take a few moments to focus on your breath, feeling the sensations of each inhale and exhale. When your mind begins to wander, gently bring your attention back to your breath. This can be done anytime, anywhere, whether you're sitting at your desk, standing in line, or walking outside.

2. Body Scan: A body scan is a technique that involves systematically bringing awareness to each part of your body, starting from the toes and working your way up to the top of your head. As you focus on each part of your body, notice any sensations or feelings that arise, without judgment or interpretation. This can help you become more aware of physical tension and release it, promoting relaxation and reducing stress.

3. Mindful Eating: Mindful eating involves paying attention to the sensory experience of eating, including the taste, smell, texture, and appearance of the food. Slow down and savor each bite, chewing slowly and fully. Notice any thoughts or emotions that arise, such as cravings or

judgments about the food, and simply observe them without getting caught up in them.

4. Mindful Walking: Mindful walking involves bringing awareness to each step as you walk, feeling the sensations in your feet and legs, and observing the environment around you. This can be done indoors or outdoors, and can be a calming and grounding practice.

5. Mindful Listening: Mindful listening involves giving your full attention to the person speaking, without judgment or distraction. Focus on the speaker's words, tone, and body language, and avoid interrupting or preparing your response while they are speaking. This can improve communication and deepen connections with others.

6. Mindful Cleaning: Cleaning can be a meditative practice when done mindfully. Focus on the sensory experience of cleaning, such as the feel of the water and the movement of your hands, rather than just trying to get the job done. This can help you stay present and calm while completing a task.

7. Mindful Resting: Taking a few moments to simply rest and be present can also be a form of mindfulness practice. Find a comfortable position and allow yourself to simply be, without the need to do anything or think about

anything. This can help reduce stress and improve overall well-being.

By incorporating these techniques into your daily life, you can cultivate a greater sense of mindfulness and presence, which can lead to greater emotional and mental well-being.

Chapter 2: Meditation
What is meditation and how does it differ from mindfulness?

Meditation is a mental practice that involves focusing one's attention on a specific object, thought, or activity to achieve a state of relaxation and mental clarity. While mindfulness is a form of meditation, it is a specific type of meditation that focuses on being present in the moment without judgment. In contrast, meditation can involve a variety of techniques, each with its own unique focus and purpose.

Meditation is a practice that has been used for thousands of years in various spiritual traditions and is now widely practiced for its numerous mental, emotional, and physical health benefits. The different types of meditation include:

1. Transcendental Meditation: This technique involves the use of a mantra or sound that is repeated silently to achieve a state of deep relaxation and inner peace.

2. Loving-Kindness Meditation: This type of meditation focuses on developing feelings of love, kindness, and compassion towards oneself and others.

3. Body Scan Meditation: This technique involves focusing on each part of the body, starting from the toes and

moving up to the head, and observing physical sensations without judgment.

4. Mindful Breathing: This technique involves paying attention to the breath and focusing on the sensation of inhaling and exhaling.

5. Vipassana Meditation: This technique is also known as insight meditation, and it involves focusing on one's thoughts and emotions without reacting to them.

The benefits of meditation for mental and emotional well-being are numerous. Regular meditation practice can help reduce stress, anxiety, and depression, improve emotional regulation, increase self-awareness, and improve overall mental clarity and cognitive functioning.

Research has shown that meditation can actually change the brain's structure and function. For example, studies have found that meditation can increase the size of the prefrontal cortex, the part of the brain responsible for decision-making, attention, and self-control. Additionally, meditation has been found to increase the thickness of the hippocampus, the part of the brain involved in memory and learning.

In summary, while mindfulness is a type of meditation that focuses on being present in the moment without judgment, there are many other forms of meditation with unique focuses and purposes. The benefits of meditation for mental and emotional well-being are numerous, and research has shown that regular meditation practice can actually change the brain's structure and function.

The benefits of meditation for mental and emotional well-being

Meditation is a practice that has been used for centuries to promote mental and emotional well-being. Recent research has confirmed that meditation can have a variety of benefits for both the mind and body. In this chapter, we will explore some of the most significant benefits of meditation for mental and emotional well-being.

1. Reduces Stress and Anxiety One of the most well-known benefits of meditation is its ability to reduce stress and anxiety. When you meditate, you activate your body's relaxation response, which helps to reduce the production of stress hormones like cortisol. Studies have shown that regular meditation practice can lead to significant reductions in symptoms of anxiety and depression.

2. Improves Emotional Well-being Meditation can also help to improve emotional well-being. By cultivating a sense of mindfulness and presence, you can become more aware of your thoughts and feelings, which can help you better understand and manage them. Meditation has been shown to reduce symptoms of depression, improve emotional regulation, and increase feelings of happiness and contentment.

3. Boosts Cognitive Functioning Research has also shown that meditation can improve cognitive functioning. Regular meditation practice has been linked to improvements in memory, attention, and decision-making. In addition, some studies have suggested that meditation can even help to slow down age-related cognitive decline.

4. Enhances Self-Awareness Meditation can help you become more self-aware by increasing your ability to reflect on your thoughts and emotions. This increased self-awareness can help you to better understand your own behavior, motivations, and patterns. By being more self-aware, you can make more intentional choices and improve your overall well-being.

5. Promotes Better Sleep Meditation can also promote better sleep by helping to regulate your body's sleep-wake cycle. When you meditate, you activate your parasympathetic nervous system, which can help you relax and fall asleep more easily. In addition, regular meditation practice has been linked to improvements in sleep quality and duration.

In conclusion, meditation can have a wide range of benefits for mental and emotional well-being. By reducing stress and anxiety, improving emotional regulation, boosting cognitive functioning, enhancing self-awareness, and promoting better sleep, meditation can help you to lead a happier, healthier, and more fulfilling life.

The science behind meditation: how it affects the brain and body

Meditation has been practiced for centuries as a way to promote inner calm and mental clarity. In recent years, modern science has begun to study the physiological and psychological effects of meditation, providing evidence for its numerous benefits on both the brain and body.

When we meditate, the brain undergoes a series of changes that can be seen in neuroimaging studies. One of the most consistent findings is that meditation increases the activity in the prefrontal cortex, the part of the brain responsible for decision-making, planning, and regulating emotions. This increased activity is thought to result in improved executive function and emotional regulation, allowing individuals to respond to stress in a more adaptive way.

Meditation has also been found to increase activity in the anterior cingulate cortex, which is involved in processing emotions and detecting errors. This increased activity is thought to lead to greater self-awareness and improved emotional regulation, allowing individuals to better understand their own emotions and respond to them in a more adaptive way.

In addition to changes in brain activity, meditation has been found to have numerous physiological benefits. For example, studies have found that regular meditation practice can reduce blood pressure and lower the levels of stress hormones such as cortisol. These effects may be due in part to the activation of the parasympathetic nervous system, which is responsible for the "rest and digest" response that counteracts the "fight or flight" response associated with stress.

Meditation has also been found to have anti-inflammatory effects, which can have a positive impact on a range of health outcomes. Chronic inflammation is thought to contribute to a wide range of diseases, including heart disease, diabetes, and some types of cancer. By reducing inflammation, meditation may help to prevent or alleviate these conditions.

Finally, meditation has been found to have a positive impact on the immune system, with regular practice being associated with increased activity of natural killer cells, which are involved in fighting infections and cancer.

Overall, the science behind meditation suggests that it can have numerous positive effects on both the brain and body, including improved emotional regulation, reduced stress and inflammation, and enhanced immune function.

Techniques for practicing meditation, including breath awareness, body scan, and loving-kindness meditation

Meditation is a practice that involves training the mind to focus and calm the thoughts, ultimately leading to a more peaceful and relaxed state of being. There are various techniques and approaches to meditation, but the following are some of the most common and effective methods.

1. Breath Awareness Meditation Breath awareness meditation is one of the simplest and most accessible forms of meditation, and it involves focusing your attention on your breath. To practice this technique, find a quiet and comfortable place to sit, either on a cushion or a chair. Close your eyes, and take a few deep breaths to relax your body. Then, bring your attention to your breath, focusing on the sensation of the air moving in and out of your body. Notice the rising and falling of your chest or abdomen as you breathe. Whenever you find your mind wandering, gently bring your focus back to your breath.

2. Body Scan Meditation Body scan meditation is a technique that involves bringing your awareness to different parts of your body, one at a time, and noticing any sensations or feelings that arise. To practice this technique, find a comfortable place to lie down or sit. Close your eyes, and

take a few deep breaths to relax your body. Then, start at the top of your head and move down through your body, paying attention to each body part in turn. Notice any areas of tension or discomfort, and try to release them through your breath.

3. Loving-Kindness Meditation Loving-kindness meditation is a technique that involves cultivating feelings of kindness, compassion, and goodwill towards yourself and others. To practice this technique, find a quiet and comfortable place to sit. Close your eyes, and take a few deep breaths to relax your body. Then, bring to mind someone you love and care for deeply. Focus on sending them feelings of love, kindness, and compassion. Repeat a phrase such as "May you be happy, healthy, and free from suffering." Then, expand this practice to include yourself, and eventually, all beings.

4. Transcendental Meditation Transcendental meditation is a technique that involves the use of a mantra, a word or phrase that is repeated silently in the mind. To practice this technique, find a quiet and comfortable place to sit. Close your eyes, and take a few deep breaths to relax your body. Then, silently repeat your chosen mantra to yourself, allowing it to fill your mind and help you to focus. Whenever

you find your mind wandering, gently bring your focus back to your mantra.

5. Movement Meditation Movement meditation is a technique that involves using movement to cultivate mindfulness and awareness. This can include practices such as yoga, tai chi, or walking meditation. To practice this technique, find a quiet and comfortable place to move. Focus your attention on the sensations of your body as you move, and try to stay present in the moment. Notice your breath, your movements, and the sensations in your body.

These techniques are just a few of the many ways to practice meditation. By experimenting with different techniques, you can find the method that works best for you and incorporate it into your daily routine. With regular practice, meditation can help to reduce stress, improve focus and concentration, and promote a sense of inner peace and well-being.

Chapter 3: Establishing a Meditation Practice
Setting up a meditation space

Setting up a dedicated meditation space can help create a sense of calm and serenity, making it easier to focus during meditation sessions. In this section, we will discuss some key considerations for setting up a meditation space that is conducive to a regular meditation practice.

Location The first consideration when setting up a meditation space is location. Ideally, you want to choose a location that is quiet, free from distractions, and where you will not be interrupted. This could be a spare room in your home, a corner of your bedroom, or even a secluded spot in your backyard. If you don't have a dedicated space available, you can also consider using a room divider or creating a makeshift meditation space with cushions and a small table.

Lighting The lighting in your meditation space should be soft and diffused, creating a calming and peaceful atmosphere. Natural light is ideal, as it can help regulate circadian rhythms and promote feelings of alertness and well-being. If natural light is not available, consider using soft, warm artificial lighting, such as lamps or candles.

Furniture and Accessories When it comes to furniture and accessories, less is often more. You want to keep your meditation space clutter-free and free from distractions. Some key items you may want to consider include:

- A meditation cushion or mat: This provides a comfortable surface to sit on during meditation sessions. You may also want to consider using a cushion or bolster to elevate your hips and facilitate good posture.

- A small table or altar: This can serve as a focal point for your practice, and you can decorate it with objects that hold personal significance or represent your spiritual beliefs.

- Incense or candles: These can help create a calming atmosphere and promote relaxation.

- Plants or flowers: These can add a natural element to your space and help purify the air.

Sound and Music Some people find that listening to calming music or sounds can enhance their meditation practice. If you choose to incorporate sound or music into your practice, make sure it is soothing and non-distracting. You may want to consider using a white noise machine or playing nature sounds to create a peaceful environment.

Creating a meditation space that is welcoming and comfortable can help you establish a regular meditation practice. Experiment with different layouts and accessories to find what works best for you. Remember, the goal is to create a space that feels calming and supportive, so you can focus on your meditation practice and cultivate a sense of inner peace and well-being.

Finding the right time of day to meditate

Meditation is a powerful tool for mental and emotional well-being, but to reap its benefits, it's important to establish a regular practice. One of the key factors in establishing a consistent practice is finding the right time of day to meditate. In this chapter, we'll explore some of the factors to consider when choosing the best time to meditate, as well as some tips for creating a regular meditation routine.

Factors to Consider When Choosing a Time to Meditate

When choosing a time to meditate, there are several factors to consider. Here are some of the most important ones:

1. Your Schedule: The first factor to consider is your schedule. If you have a busy schedule, it may be challenging to find time to meditate during the day. However, if you're willing to make meditation a priority, you can often find ways to fit it into your day. For example, you may be able to wake up earlier in the morning to meditate, or you may be able to meditate during your lunch break or in the evening.

2. Your Energy Levels: Another factor to consider is your energy levels. Some people find that they have more energy in the morning and prefer to meditate first thing when they wake up. Others find that they have more energy

in the afternoon or evening and prefer to meditate during those times.

3. Your Environment: The environment in which you meditate can also be an important factor. If you live in a busy household, for example, you may find it challenging to meditate when there are lots of people around. If this is the case, you may want to consider meditating early in the morning or late at night when the house is quieter.

4. Your Goals: Finally, your meditation goals can also influence the best time of day to meditate. For example, if you're using meditation to help you fall asleep, you may want to meditate just before bed. If you're using meditation to help you focus and increase productivity, you may want to meditate in the morning to start your day off on the right foot.

Tips for Establishing a Regular Meditation Routine

Once you've chosen a time to meditate, the next step is to establish a regular routine. Here are some tips for creating a consistent meditation practice:

1. Start Small: When you're just getting started with meditation, it's important to start small. Begin with just a few minutes of meditation each day and gradually increase the length of your sessions as you become more comfortable with the practice.

2. Create a Ritual: Creating a ritual around your meditation practice can help to make it feel more meaningful and enjoyable. This could involve lighting a candle, burning some incense, or playing some relaxing music.

3. Use Guided Meditations: If you're having trouble staying focused during your meditation sessions, using guided meditations can be helpful. There are many guided meditation apps and websites available that can help to guide you through the practice.

4. Hold Yourself Accountable: Finally, it's important to hold yourself accountable for your meditation practice. Set a goal to meditate for a certain amount of time each day, and track your progress in a journal or on a meditation app. Having a sense of accountability can help you to stay motivated and committed to your practice.

In conclusion, finding the right time of day to meditate is an important factor in establishing a regular meditation practice. By considering your schedule, energy levels, environment, and goals, you can choose a time that works best for you. And by starting small, creating a ritual, using guided meditations, and holding yourself accountable, you can establish a consistent meditation routine that can help to improve your mental and emotional well-being.

Developing a regular meditation practice

Developing a regular meditation practice can be a challenging task, especially for those who are new to meditation. However, with dedication and practice, it is possible to establish a regular meditation practice that becomes a daily habit. In this section, we will discuss some tips for developing a regular meditation practice.

1. Start small

When beginning a meditation practice, it is important to start small. Many people find it challenging to sit for an extended period of time, so it is best to start with just a few minutes of meditation each day. Over time, you can gradually increase the amount of time you spend in meditation.

2. Choose a specific time of day

It can be helpful to choose a specific time of day to meditate, such as first thing in the morning or before bedtime. By establishing a regular routine, you are more likely to stick with your practice.

3. Create a dedicated space

Having a dedicated space for meditation can help to create a peaceful and calming environment. This space can be as simple as a corner of your bedroom or a specific cushion or chair that you use only for meditation.

4. Use guided meditations

Guided meditations can be a helpful tool for those who are new to meditation. There are many apps and online resources that offer guided meditations for free. These guided meditations can help to provide structure and focus during your practice.

5. Set realistic goals

It is important to set realistic goals for your meditation practice. Don't expect to become an expert meditator overnight. Instead, focus on establishing a regular practice and gradually improving your skills over time.

6. Be consistent

Consistency is key when developing a regular meditation practice. Try to meditate at the same time every day, and make it a non-negotiable part of your routine. By making meditation a priority, you are more likely to stick with it.

7. Practice self-compassion

Finally, it is important to practice self-compassion when developing a regular meditation practice. Don't beat yourself up if you miss a day or struggle with your practice. Be kind to yourself, and remember that meditation is a lifelong journey.

By following these tips, you can establish a regular meditation practice that becomes a daily habit. With time and practice, you will begin to experience the many benefits of meditation, including improved focus, reduced stress, and greater emotional well-being.

Overcoming common challenges in meditation

Meditation is a powerful tool for cultivating mindfulness, reducing stress, and promoting emotional well-being. However, many people struggle with establishing a regular meditation practice due to a variety of challenges. In this section, we will discuss some of the most common challenges that people face when trying to meditate, and offer strategies for overcoming them.

1. Difficulty focusing: One of the biggest challenges in meditation is maintaining focus. The mind has a natural tendency to wander, and many people find it difficult to keep their attention on their breath or other focal point. However, with regular practice, it is possible to strengthen the mind's ability to concentrate. Here are a few tips for overcoming difficulty focusing:

- Start with short meditation sessions: If you're new to meditation, start with just a few minutes of practice each day, and gradually increase the duration as you become more comfortable.

- Use guided meditations: Guided meditations can be helpful for keeping your attention focused, as they provide a clear structure and guidance throughout the practice.

- Practice with a group: Meditating with others can be a powerful way to stay focused and motivated. Consider joining a meditation group or attending a retreat.

- Practice mindfulness throughout the day: You can also cultivate mindfulness throughout the day by paying attention to your thoughts, emotions, and sensations as they arise. This can help strengthen your overall ability to focus.

2. Physical discomfort: Sitting in one position for an extended period of time can be physically challenging, especially if you're not used to it. Here are a few tips for overcoming physical discomfort:

- Experiment with different positions: You don't have to sit cross-legged on the floor to meditate. Try sitting on a cushion, a chair, or even lying down.

- Use props: Props like cushions, blankets, and blocks can help support your body and make it easier to sit comfortably.

- Take breaks: If you're feeling uncomfortable, take a break and stretch or walk around for a few minutes before returning to your practice.

- Practice yoga or other physical activity: Regular physical activity can help prepare your body for meditation by improving flexibility and reducing tension.

3. Resistance to meditation: Many people struggle with resistance to meditation, either because they find it boring, or because they're afraid of what they might uncover through introspection. Here are a few tips for overcoming resistance:

- Set a clear intention: Before each meditation session, set a clear intention for why you're practicing. This can help you stay focused and motivated.

- Be gentle with yourself: Don't judge yourself if your mind wanders or if you feel resistance. Instead, simply acknowledge the experience and gently guide your attention back to your focal point.

- Explore your resistance: If you find yourself consistently avoiding meditation, take some time to explore why. Are there underlying beliefs or fears that are holding you back? By bringing awareness to these barriers, you can begin to work through them.

- Practice self-compassion: Remember that meditation is a practice, and that it's okay to struggle with it. Be kind and compassionate with yourself, and celebrate your progress along the way.

In summary, establishing a regular meditation practice can be challenging, but it is also incredibly rewarding. By developing strategies for overcoming common challenges, you can build a sustainable practice that promotes mental and emotional well-being.

Chapter 4: Mindfulness-Based Stress Reduction
The connection between stress and mental health

Stress is a natural response of the body to a perceived threat or challenge. When we encounter stressors, whether physical, emotional, or mental, the body's stress response is triggered, releasing a cascade of hormones and chemicals, such as adrenaline, cortisol, and norepinephrine, into the bloodstream. These chemicals prepare the body for the "fight or flight" response, allowing us to respond to the stressor with increased alertness, energy, and focus.

In small doses, stress can be helpful, helping us to perform better under pressure and meet deadlines. However, chronic stress, or stress that persists over a long period of time, can have negative effects on our mental and physical health. Chronic stress can weaken the immune system, increase the risk of cardiovascular disease, and exacerbate mental health conditions such as anxiety and depression.

Stress can come from a variety of sources, including work, relationships, financial concerns, health issues, and daily hassles. In today's fast-paced world, many people experience high levels of stress on a regular basis, which can lead to a range of negative outcomes. For example, chronic stress can cause burnout, a state of emotional, physical, and mental exhaustion that can make it difficult to function and enjoy life.

To mitigate the negative effects of stress, it is important to develop effective coping strategies. Mindfulness-Based Stress Reduction (MBSR) is a program that has been shown to be effective in reducing stress and improving mental and physical health outcomes.

MBSR was developed in the 1970s by Jon Kabat-Zinn at the University of Massachusetts Medical School. The program combines mindfulness meditation, body awareness, and yoga to help individuals reduce stress and improve their overall well-being. The program is typically taught in an eight-week course and includes weekly group sessions and daily home practice.

Research has shown that MBSR can be effective in reducing symptoms of stress, anxiety, and depression. Studies have also found that MBSR can improve immune function, decrease inflammation, and reduce the risk of chronic diseases such as heart disease and diabetes.

In addition to reducing stress and improving physical health outcomes, MBSR can also help individuals develop a greater sense of self-awareness and emotional regulation. By learning to be present with their thoughts, feelings, and bodily sensations, individuals can develop greater insight into their patterns of thinking and behavior, and learn to respond to stressors in a more effective and adaptive way.

Overall, stress is a common experience in modern life, and chronic stress can have negative effects on our mental and physical health. MBSR is a program that has been shown to be effective in reducing stress and improving overall well-being. By combining mindfulness meditation, body awareness, and yoga, individuals can learn to develop greater self-awareness and emotional regulation, leading to improved mental and physical health outcomes.

How mindfulness can reduce stress

Mindfulness-Based Stress Reduction (MBSR) is an evidence-based program that teaches individuals how to use mindfulness practices to reduce stress and improve well-being. Mindfulness meditation is a key component of MBSR, which teaches participants to focus on the present moment and develop a non-judgmental awareness of their thoughts, feelings, and bodily sensations.

MBSR has been shown to be effective in reducing stress and improving physical and mental health outcomes. In this chapter, we will explore the connection between stress and mental health and how mindfulness can reduce stress.

Stress and Mental Health

Stress is a normal response to challenging situations, such as work deadlines, financial problems, or relationship conflicts. When the body perceives a threat, it triggers the "fight or flight" response, which activates the sympathetic nervous system and releases hormones such as cortisol and adrenaline. These hormones increase heart rate, blood pressure, and respiration, preparing the body to respond to the threat.

While stress can be helpful in short-term situations, chronic stress can have negative effects on physical and mental health. Chronic stress can lead to increased risk of heart disease, stroke, and other chronic conditions. It can also contribute to mental health problems such as anxiety and depression.

How Mindfulness Reduces Stress

Mindfulness can be a powerful tool in reducing stress because it helps individuals become more aware of their thoughts and emotions and develop a more accepting and compassionate attitude toward themselves. Mindfulness meditation teaches individuals to focus on the present moment and develop a non-judgmental awareness of their thoughts, feelings, and bodily sensations.

When practicing mindfulness, individuals learn to observe their thoughts and emotions without getting caught up in them. This helps to reduce the intensity and frequency of negative thoughts and emotions, which can contribute to stress.

Mindfulness also helps individuals develop a more accepting and compassionate attitude toward themselves. This can reduce self-criticism and self-judgment, which can be a source of stress. When individuals learn to accept and love themselves for who they are, they can become more resilient in the face of stress.

Research has shown that mindfulness can reduce the symptoms of stress, anxiety, and depression. In one study, individuals who participated in an eight-week MBSR program reported significant reductions in stress and anxiety compared to a control group (1). Another study found that mindfulness meditation was effective in reducing symptoms of depression in individuals with chronic pain (2).

Conclusion

Stress can have negative effects on physical and mental health, but mindfulness can be a powerful tool in reducing stress. Mindfulness meditation teaches individuals to focus on the present moment and develop a non-judgmental awareness of their thoughts, feelings, and bodily sensations. This can help individuals become more aware of their stress triggers and develop a more accepting and compassionate attitude toward themselves. MBSR is an evidence-based program that can teach individuals how to use mindfulness practices to reduce stress and improve well-being.

Techniques for using mindfulness to manage stress in daily life

Mindfulness-Based Stress Reduction (MBSR) is a well-known program that incorporates mindfulness practices into stress management techniques. It was developed by Dr. Jon Kabat-Zinn in the 1970s to help patients with chronic pain, and it has since been used to help people manage stress, anxiety, and depression.

The techniques used in MBSR are designed to help individuals become more aware of their thoughts, feelings, and bodily sensations. By cultivating this awareness, individuals can learn to identify their stress triggers and manage their stress more effectively. The following are some mindfulness techniques that can be used to manage stress in daily life:

1. Mindful breathing: Mindful breathing is a simple technique that involves focusing your attention on your breath. You can practice mindful breathing by finding a quiet place to sit or lie down and then focusing your attention on your breath as it moves in and out of your body. If your mind wanders, simply bring your attention back to your breath.

2. Body scan: The body scan is a mindfulness technique that involves bringing your attention to different parts of your body. You can practice the body scan by lying

down on your back and bringing your attention to your toes. Slowly move your attention up your body, paying attention to each part of your body as you go.

3. Mindful walking: Mindful walking is a technique that involves bringing your attention to your body as you walk. You can practice mindful walking by walking slowly and deliberately, paying attention to the way your body moves as you walk.

4. Mindful eating: Mindful eating is a technique that involves bringing your attention to your food as you eat it. You can practice mindful eating by focusing on the texture, taste, and smell of your food as you eat it.

5. Loving-kindness meditation: Loving-kindness meditation is a technique that involves cultivating feelings of love, kindness, and compassion towards yourself and others. You can practice loving-kindness meditation by sitting in a quiet place and repeating phrases such as "May I be happy," "May I be healthy," "May I be safe," "May I live with ease."

6. Mindful journaling: Mindful journaling is a technique that involves writing down your thoughts and feelings in a non-judgmental way. You can practice mindful journaling by finding a quiet place to write and then writing down your thoughts and feelings as they come up.

These techniques can be practiced individually or in combination with one another. By incorporating mindfulness techniques into your daily routine, you can learn to manage your stress more effectively and improve your overall mental and emotional well-being.

Mindful breathing exercises and body scans

Mindful breathing exercises and body scans are two powerful mindfulness techniques that can be used to manage stress and improve overall well-being. Both techniques are relatively easy to learn and can be practiced almost anywhere, making them perfect for integrating into a busy daily routine.

Mindful Breathing Exercises

Mindful breathing exercises are one of the most basic and effective techniques for reducing stress and promoting relaxation. The goal of mindful breathing is to focus the mind on the breath, allowing all other thoughts and distractions to fade away. Mindful breathing can be practiced in several different ways, including:

1. Counting breaths: One simple way to practice mindful breathing is to count each breath as it enters and leaves the body. Start by sitting in a comfortable position with your eyes closed. Take a few deep breaths, then begin counting each inhale and exhale, starting with one and counting up to ten. If your mind wanders, simply bring your attention back to the breath and start counting again from one.

2. Belly breathing: Belly breathing, also known as diaphragmatic breathing, is a technique that involves taking

slow, deep breaths that expand the belly rather than the chest. This technique is particularly helpful for calming the nervous system and reducing stress. To practice belly breathing, sit in a comfortable position with your hands on your belly. Inhale slowly through your nose, feeling your belly expand as you breathe in. Hold the breath for a few seconds, then exhale slowly through your mouth, feeling your belly contract as you breathe out.

3. Breath awareness: Breath awareness is a technique that involves simply observing the breath without trying to change it in any way. To practice breath awareness, sit in a comfortable position and bring your attention to your breath. Notice the sensation of the breath as it enters and leaves your body, without judging or analyzing it. If your mind wanders, gently bring your attention back to the breath.

Body Scans

Body scans are another mindfulness technique that can help to reduce stress and promote relaxation. A body scan involves systematically bringing awareness to each part of the body, from the top of the head down to the toes. The goal of a body scan is to become aware of any areas of tension or discomfort in the body, and to release that tension through deep breathing and relaxation.

To practice a body scan, find a quiet and comfortable place to lie down or sit. Close your eyes and bring your attention to your breath for a few moments, then begin to scan through your body from the top of the head down to the toes. As you focus on each part of the body, notice any sensations that arise, such as tension or discomfort. Take a few deep breaths, imagining that you are sending relaxation and healing to that area of the body. As you move through each part of the body, allow yourself to relax more and more deeply.

Conclusion

Mindful breathing exercises and body scans are powerful tools for reducing stress, promoting relaxation, and improving overall well-being. These techniques can be practiced almost anywhere, making them perfect for integrating into a busy daily routine. By making mindfulness a part of your daily life, you can learn to manage stress more effectively and cultivate a greater sense of calm and balance.

Chapter 5: Mindfulness and Relationships
How mindfulness can improve relationships

Mindfulness is not only beneficial for personal well-being but also has positive effects on relationships with others. In fact, research suggests that mindfulness can improve relationship satisfaction, communication, and overall well-being of both partners.

In this chapter, we will explore how mindfulness can improve relationships and provide some practical techniques for incorporating mindfulness into your relationships.

What is Mindful Relationship?

Mindful relationships are those in which both partners practice mindfulness together, communicating with each other in a conscious and present manner. Mindful relationships involve being fully present and engaged with your partner in a non-judgmental way. It involves acknowledging your thoughts and feelings without getting caught up in them, and actively listening to your partner without reacting or becoming defensive.

Benefits of Mindful Relationships

1. Improved Communication: Mindfulness can help partners communicate more effectively by increasing their awareness of their thoughts, emotions, and behaviors. When partners are mindful, they are better able to listen and

respond to each other in a non-judgmental way, leading to improved communication and understanding.

2. Increased Empathy and Compassion: Mindfulness helps partners to develop empathy and compassion towards each other by helping them to understand each other's perspectives and experiences. When partners are able to view things from each other's point of view, they are better able to empathize and connect with each other.

3. Greater Relationship Satisfaction: Mindful partners report greater relationship satisfaction and intimacy. When partners are mindful, they are better able to connect with each other on a deeper level, leading to a greater sense of closeness and intimacy.

4. Reduced Stress and Conflict: Mindful partners report reduced stress and conflict in their relationships. When partners are mindful, they are better able to manage their emotions and respond to each other in a calm and non-reactive manner, reducing the likelihood of conflict and stress.

Techniques for Incorporating Mindfulness into Relationships

1. Mindful Listening: Mindful listening involves being fully present and engaged with your partner when they are speaking, without interrupting or becoming distracted. To

practice mindful listening, focus on your partner's words and non-verbal cues, and acknowledge their thoughts and feelings without judgment.

2. Mindful Breathing: Mindful breathing is a simple and effective way to bring mindfulness into your relationship. Take a few deep breaths before engaging with your partner to help calm your mind and increase your focus.

3. Mindful Touch: Mindful touch involves being present and focused during physical contact with your partner. Whether it's holding hands, hugging, or kissing, try to focus on the physical sensations and emotions that arise during the interaction.

4. Mindful Eating: Mindful eating involves paying attention to the food you are consuming, the taste, smell, and texture of the food, and the experience of eating with your partner. This technique can help you and your partner to connect on a deeper level and increase your sense of intimacy.

5. Mindful Conflict Resolution: Mindful conflict resolution involves approaching conflicts in a calm and non-reactive way. Rather than getting defensive or angry, try to remain present and focused, acknowledging your own thoughts and feelings, as well as your partner's, in a non-

judgmental way. This approach can help you to resolve conflicts more effectively and strengthen your relationship.

Conclusion

Mindfulness can improve relationships in many ways, including improving communication, increasing empathy and compassion, and reducing stress and conflict. By incorporating mindfulness techniques into your relationships, you can develop a deeper sense of connection and intimacy with your partner, leading to greater relationship satisfaction and overall well-being.

Mindful communication

Effective communication is crucial in building and maintaining healthy relationships, whether they are personal or professional. Mindful communication is a way of expressing ourselves that focuses on being present and attentive to the person we are communicating with, without judgment or bias. In this chapter, we will explore the principles and techniques of mindful communication and how it can improve our relationships.

What is Mindful Communication?

Mindful communication is a form of communication that is grounded in mindfulness practice. It involves being present and attentive to the person we are communicating with, without judgment or bias. Mindful communication requires us to listen deeply to the other person, to understand their perspective and feelings, and to respond in a way that is compassionate and respectful.

Principles of Mindful Communication:

1. Presence: Mindful communication requires us to be fully present in the moment, with an open and curious attitude.

2. Non-judgment: Mindful communication involves suspending judgment and assumptions about the other person's thoughts or feelings.

3. Compassion: Mindful communication is rooted in a spirit of kindness and compassion towards ourselves and others.

4. Clarity: Mindful communication involves being clear and concise in our communication, avoiding ambiguity and confusion.

Techniques for Mindful Communication:

1. Active Listening: Active listening involves giving our full attention to the other person, without interrupting or formulating responses in our head. It requires us to be fully present, to ask clarifying questions, and to reflect back what we have heard.

2. Nonviolent Communication (NVC): NVC is a communication process developed by psychologist Marshall Rosenberg that emphasizes compassion and empathy. It involves expressing ourselves in a way that is honest and respectful, while also being attuned to the other person's feelings and needs.

3. Mindful Speaking: Mindful speaking involves being aware of our words and tone of voice, and expressing ourselves in a way that is clear and compassionate. It requires us to take a moment to reflect on what we want to say, and to consider how it might be received by the other person.

Benefits of Mindful Communication:

1. Improved Relationships: Mindful communication can help us build and maintain healthy relationships with others, by fostering understanding, empathy, and mutual respect.

2. Reduced Conflict: Mindful communication can help us resolve conflicts in a way that is compassionate and respectful, rather than adversarial.

3. Enhanced Self-Awareness: Mindful communication can also help us become more aware of our own thoughts and feelings, and how they influence our communication with others.

Conclusion:

Mindful communication is an essential tool for building and maintaining healthy relationships. By practicing mindful communication, we can learn to listen more deeply, express ourselves more clearly, and develop greater empathy and understanding for others. By cultivating these skills, we can enhance our personal and professional relationships, and foster greater harmony and well-being in our lives.

Active listening

Active listening is an essential skill in any relationship, but it can be challenging to practice, especially when emotions are running high. It involves not just hearing the words someone is saying but also understanding their meaning and empathizing with their perspective. When we practice active listening, we create a safe space for the other person to express themselves and feel heard and understood, which can foster greater trust and connection in our relationships.

Here are some techniques for practicing active listening with mindfulness:

1. Pay attention to body language: Nonverbal cues can reveal a lot about how someone is feeling, often more than their words. Pay attention to their facial expressions, posture, and gestures, and try to empathize with how they might be feeling based on their body language.

2. Avoid interrupting: Interrupting someone when they are speaking can be frustrating and can disrupt the flow of the conversation. Instead, practice patience and allow them to finish their thoughts before responding.

3. Listen without judgment: It's easy to jump to conclusions or make assumptions about what someone is saying, but this can interfere with truly understanding their

perspective. Try to listen without judgment or preconceptions, and keep an open mind.

4. Reflect back what you heard: To ensure that you understand what the other person is saying, reflect back what you heard in your own words. This can also help to clarify any misunderstandings and ensure that you're on the same page.

5. Ask questions: Asking questions can show that you're engaged and interested in what the other person is saying. It can also help to clarify any points that you're unsure of and encourage the other person to elaborate on their thoughts and feelings.

6. Practice mindful breathing: If you find yourself getting distracted or agitated during a conversation, take a few deep breaths to ground yourself in the present moment. This can help you stay focused and centered, even in challenging conversations.

By practicing active listening with mindfulness, we can cultivate deeper and more meaningful connections in our relationships. We can learn to empathize with others, communicate more effectively, and create a safe and supportive space for everyone to express themselves.

Developing empathy and compassion

Developing empathy and compassion is an essential part of improving relationships and fostering connection with others. Mindfulness can be a powerful tool for cultivating these qualities, as it helps individuals become more aware of their own thoughts and emotions, as well as those of others. In this section, we will explore the science behind empathy and compassion and provide practical techniques for developing these qualities through mindfulness practice.

The Science of Empathy and Compassion

Empathy is the ability to understand and share the feelings of others. It involves tuning in to the emotional states of others and being able to perceive their experiences from their perspective. Compassion, on the other hand, involves feeling a deep sense of concern and care for the well-being of others, especially when they are experiencing pain or suffering. While empathy and compassion are related, they are distinct qualities that involve different brain processes.

Research has shown that when individuals practice mindfulness, they become more attuned to the emotional states of others. Specifically, mindfulness has been found to increase activity in the anterior insula, a brain region that plays a key role in empathy. This increased activity may make individuals more sensitive to the emotions of others and better able to respond with compassion.

In addition to these neurological changes, mindfulness also appears to have a positive effect on social behavior. Studies have found that individuals who practice mindfulness are more likely to engage in prosocial behaviors, such as volunteering, donating to charity, and offering emotional support to others. This may be due in part to the increased feelings of empathy and compassion that mindfulness cultivates.

Techniques for Developing Empathy and Compassion

1. Loving-Kindness Meditation

Loving-kindness meditation is a mindfulness practice that involves sending well wishes to oneself and others. This practice has been found to increase feelings of compassion and empathy towards oneself and others, as well as reduce feelings of stress and anxiety. To practice loving-kindness meditation, find a quiet place where you can sit comfortably for a few minutes. Close your eyes and take a few deep breaths. Then, repeat the following phrases silently to yourself, directing them first towards yourself, then towards a loved one, a neutral person, a difficult person, and all beings:

May I/you/he/she/they be happy. May I/you/he/she/they be healthy. May I/you/he/she/they be safe. May I/you/he/she/they live with ease.

2. Compassionate Listening

Compassionate listening is a technique for improving communication and fostering empathy with others. It involves actively listening to the experiences and feelings of another person without judgment or interruption. To practice compassionate listening, find a quiet place where you can sit comfortably with another person. Set a timer for five minutes and take turns speaking and listening. When it is your turn to listen, focus your attention on the other person's words and try to understand their perspective without judgment. When it is your turn to speak, try to express your own feelings and experiences in a clear and non-judgmental way.

3. Mindful Breathing

Mindful breathing is a technique that involves paying close attention to the sensations of the breath as it moves in and out of the body. This practice can help individuals become more grounded and centered, which can in turn increase feelings of empathy and compassion towards oneself and others. To practice mindful breathing, find a quiet place where you can sit comfortably for a few minutes.

Close your eyes and take a few deep breaths. Then, begin to focus your attention on the sensation of the breath as it moves in and out of the body. You may choose to focus on the sensation of the breath at the nostrils, the chest, or the abdomen.

In conclusion, developing empathy and compassion is an important aspect of improving relationships and fostering connection with others. Mindfulness can be an effective tool for cultivating these qualities, as it helps individuals become more aware of their own thoughts, feelings, and behaviors, which can then extend to being more attuned to the experiences of others. By practicing mindfulness, individuals can develop a greater capacity for empathy and compassion, which can lead to more fulfilling and satisfying relationships. Additionally, research has shown that mindfulness-based interventions can increase levels of empathy and compassion in both clinical and non-clinical populations, suggesting that these practices can have a positive impact on interpersonal relationships.

One way to develop empathy and compassion through mindfulness is by practicing loving-kindness meditation. This practice involves directing well-wishes towards oneself and others, with the intention of cultivating feelings of love, kindness, and compassion. Through this practice, individuals can learn to extend care and concern towards themselves and others, even in difficult situations. Another way to develop empathy and compassion is by practicing non-judgmental awareness of thoughts and emotions. By learning to observe thoughts and emotions without judgment, individuals can gain a greater understanding of their own internal experiences, which can then extend to being more attuned to the experiences of others. Additionally, practicing gratitude and acts of kindness towards others can help individuals develop a greater sense of connection and compassion towards others.

Overall, developing empathy and compassion through mindfulness practices can lead to more fulfilling and satisfying relationships. By becoming more attuned to the experiences of others and developing a greater capacity for care and concern, individuals can create deeper connections and foster greater intimacy in their relationships.

Chapter 6: Mindfulness and Productivity
How mindfulness can improve productivity

In today's fast-paced world, productivity has become a key factor in achieving success in various areas of life, from work to personal projects. However, with increasing distractions and a constant stream of information, it can be challenging to maintain focus and accomplish our goals. This is where mindfulness can come in to help.

Mindfulness is the practice of being present and fully engaged in the current moment, without judgment or distraction. It involves paying attention to one's thoughts, feelings, and surroundings, with a sense of openness and curiosity. By practicing mindfulness, individuals can learn to better regulate their attention and emotions, which can lead to increased productivity and efficiency.

One way mindfulness can improve productivity is by reducing stress levels. When individuals are stressed, they are more likely to feel overwhelmed, anxious, and distracted, which can negatively impact their ability to focus and get things done. Mindfulness can help reduce stress by promoting relaxation and calming the mind, which can improve concentration and clarity of thought.

In addition, mindfulness can also enhance creativity and problem-solving skills. By cultivating a non-judgmental attitude and being open to new ideas, individuals can approach challenges with a fresh perspective and generate innovative solutions. This can lead to increased efficiency and better outcomes.

Moreover, mindfulness can also help individuals prioritize their tasks and manage their time more effectively. By being more aware of their thoughts and feelings, individuals can identify what tasks are most important and allocate their time accordingly. This can help prevent procrastination and increase motivation to accomplish goals.

Furthermore, mindfulness can also improve communication and collaboration skills, which are essential for productivity in many settings, such as the workplace. By being more attentive and present in interactions with others, individuals can better understand their needs and perspectives, and work together more effectively towards shared goals.

In summary, mindfulness can improve productivity by reducing stress, enhancing creativity and problem-solving skills, helping individuals prioritize tasks and manage time more effectively, and improving communication and collaboration skills. By incorporating mindfulness practices into daily routines, individuals can cultivate a more focused, productive, and fulfilling life.

Techniques for practicing mindfulness in the workplace

In today's fast-paced work culture, it's common for individuals to feel overwhelmed and stressed. Mindfulness can help employees manage their stress levels and improve productivity. By focusing on the present moment, employees can remain calm and centered, allowing them to be more productive and efficient. In this section, we'll explore some techniques for practicing mindfulness in the workplace.

1. Mindful breathing exercises: Taking a few minutes to focus on your breath can help you calm your mind and reduce stress. You can practice mindful breathing exercises at your desk, in a meeting room, or even during a break. Simply close your eyes and take a few deep breaths, paying attention to the sensation of the breath moving in and out of your body. If your mind starts to wander, gently bring your attention back to your breath.

2. Body scan meditation: Body scan meditation involves systematically scanning through your body, paying attention to any areas of tension or discomfort. This practice can help you become more aware of physical sensations and can help you release tension and stress. You can do a quick body scan at your desk, or take a few minutes in a quiet room to do a more thorough scan.

3. Mindful walking: If you have the opportunity to take a short break, consider going for a mindful walk. As you walk, pay attention to the sensation of your feet touching the ground and the movement of your body. Try to focus on the present moment and let go of any distracting thoughts.

4. Mindful eating: Eating mindfully involves paying close attention to the experience of eating, including the taste, texture, and smell of the food. By eating mindfully, you can enjoy your food more fully and can also be more aware of when you're full, which can help you avoid overeating.

5. Mindful breaks: Taking short breaks throughout the day can help you stay focused and energized. During your breaks, try to engage in activities that help you relax and recharge. This might include reading, listening to music, or simply sitting quietly and focusing on your breath.

6. Mindful meetings: Mindful meetings involve being fully present and engaged during meetings. This means actively listening to others, avoiding distractions, and participating in the discussion. By practicing mindfulness during meetings, you can improve communication and collaboration with your colleagues.

Incorporating mindfulness into your workday can help you stay focused, manage stress, and improve productivity. By taking a few moments to practice mindfulness throughout the day, you can create a more balanced and fulfilling work life.

Overcoming distractions and staying focused

In today's fast-paced work environment, distractions are everywhere, and staying focused on tasks can be a real challenge. Mindfulness can help individuals overcome these distractions and stay focused on the task at hand. Here are some techniques for practicing mindfulness to overcome distractions and improve productivity in the workplace:

1. Minimize distractions: Minimizing distractions can be an effective way to stay focused. This can include turning off notifications on your phone or computer, closing unnecessary tabs, and finding a quiet space to work.

2. Practice single-tasking: Instead of trying to juggle multiple tasks simultaneously, try focusing on one task at a time. This can help you stay present and engaged with the task, ultimately leading to better results.

3. Take mindful breaks: Taking breaks can actually increase productivity, as it allows the mind to rest and recharge. Taking mindful breaks, such as a brief walk outside or a few minutes of meditation, can be particularly effective in reducing stress and improving focus.

4. Use mindfulness techniques to handle stress: Stress is a major distraction in the workplace, and it can significantly impact productivity. Mindfulness techniques

such as deep breathing, body scans, and visualization can help manage stress and improve focus.

5. Practice self-compassion: It's important to remember that distractions and setbacks are a natural part of the workday. Practicing self-compassion can help you stay motivated and focused, even in the face of challenges.

By incorporating these techniques into their daily routine, individuals can overcome distractions and stay focused on their work, ultimately leading to increased productivity and better outcomes.

Using mindfulness to prioritize tasks

In today's fast-paced world, we often have too many tasks to complete in too little time. This can lead to stress, anxiety, and a feeling of overwhelm. However, by practicing mindfulness, we can learn to prioritize our tasks and get more done with less stress.

Here are some techniques for using mindfulness to prioritize tasks:

1. Take a step back: When you're feeling overwhelmed, take a step back and take a few deep breaths. This can help you to clear your mind and focus on what's most important.

2. Evaluate your tasks: Take a look at your to-do list and evaluate each task. Ask yourself, "Is this task really important?" If the task is not important, consider removing it from your list.

3. Identify urgent tasks: Identify the tasks that are most urgent and require immediate attention. These tasks should be your top priority.

4. Break down large tasks: If you have a large task on your to-do list, break it down into smaller, more manageable tasks. This can make the task seem less daunting and help you to stay focused.

5. Use the 80/20 rule: The 80/20 rule states that 80% of your results come from 20% of your efforts. Identify the tasks that are most important and focus on those first.

6. Practice single-tasking: Instead of trying to do multiple things at once, practice single-tasking. Focus on one task at a time and give it your full attention.

7. Use a task management tool: Consider using a task management tool, such as Trello or Asana, to help you stay organized and prioritize your tasks.

8. Prioritize self-care: Remember to prioritize self-care and make time for activities that help you to relax and recharge. When you take care of yourself, you'll be better equipped to handle the tasks on your to-do list.

By using these techniques, you can learn to prioritize your tasks and get more done with less stress. Remember, mindfulness is a practice, so be patient with yourself and keep practicing. With time and consistency, you'll find that mindfulness becomes a natural part of your daily routine.

Chapter 7: Mindfulness and Self-Compassion
How mindfulness can help develop self-compassion

Self-compassion refers to treating oneself with kindness, care, and understanding when faced with difficult experiences or personal shortcomings. It is an essential aspect of psychological well-being and resilience. However, many people struggle with self-compassion, often being their harshest critic and lacking self-acceptance. Fortunately, mindfulness can help cultivate self-compassion by allowing individuals to approach their inner experiences with curiosity, openness, and non-judgment.

Mindfulness encourages individuals to pay attention to their thoughts, feelings, and bodily sensations with an attitude of curiosity and non-judgment. By cultivating this kind of self-awareness, people can become more attuned to their inner experiences, including negative emotions and self-criticism. Rather than trying to push these thoughts and feelings away, mindfulness encourages individuals to acknowledge and accept them, providing an opportunity for greater self-understanding and self-compassion.

One way mindfulness can help develop self-compassion is through the practice of self-compassion meditation. This type of meditation involves directing loving-kindness and compassion towards oneself, just as one would towards a loved one or friend. During this practice, individuals repeat phrases such as "May I be happy" or "May I be kind to myself," allowing them to cultivate positive feelings towards themselves and increase self-compassion.

Another way mindfulness can help develop self-compassion is through cultivating a non-judgmental attitude towards oneself. Often, people are their harshest critic and judge themselves harshly for their mistakes and shortcomings. Mindfulness can help individuals recognize their self-judgment and develop a more compassionate and accepting attitude towards themselves. This allows them to view themselves with greater kindness and understanding, promoting self-compassion.

Moreover, mindfulness can help individuals develop greater resilience in the face of difficult experiences. By cultivating mindfulness and self-compassion, individuals can develop a more positive attitude towards themselves, promoting greater psychological well-being and resilience.

In conclusion, mindfulness can help cultivate self-compassion by encouraging individuals to approach their inner experiences with curiosity, openness, and non-judgment. By developing greater self-awareness and self-acceptance, people can increase their self-compassion, promoting greater psychological well-being and resilience.

Practicing self-compassion in daily life

Self-compassion is the practice of being kind, supportive, and understanding towards oneself. It involves treating oneself with the same level of care and concern that one would offer to a good friend. In contrast to self-esteem, which involves evaluating oneself positively and feeling good about one's accomplishments, self-compassion involves accepting oneself, flaws and all, and recognizing that suffering is a normal part of the human experience. Mindfulness can be a powerful tool in cultivating self-compassion, as it allows individuals to observe their thoughts and emotions without judgment, which can lead to greater self-awareness and self-acceptance.

Here are some techniques for practicing self-compassion in daily life:

1. Self-Compassion Breaks: This technique involves taking a moment to acknowledge and validate one's own suffering, and offering oneself words of kindness and support. It can be done by pausing for a few moments, taking a deep breath, and repeating phrases such as "May I be kind to myself", "May I give myself the compassion I need", or "May I accept myself just as I am."

2. Mindful Self-Compassion Meditation: This practice involves sitting quietly and focusing on the breath, while also

bringing awareness to any physical or emotional discomfort. One can then offer oneself words of kindness and support, such as "May I be gentle with myself", "May I give myself the care I need", or "May I be patient with my struggles."

3. Daily Gratitude Practice: Practicing gratitude can help shift one's focus away from negative thoughts and feelings and towards a more positive and compassionate mindset. Take a few moments each day to reflect on what you are grateful for, and try to focus on the small things in life that bring joy and happiness.

4. Compassionate Self-Talk: Be aware of how you talk to yourself, and try to reframe negative self-talk in a more compassionate way. For example, if you make a mistake at work, instead of beating yourself up with thoughts like "I'm such an idiot", try reframing the thought to "Mistakes happen, and I'm doing the best I can."

5. Mindful Movement: Engage in physical activities that promote mindfulness, such as yoga or tai chi. These practices can help cultivate a sense of awareness and acceptance of one's body, and can also be a way to connect with others who share similar values.

Overall, practicing self-compassion requires patience, persistence, and a willingness to be vulnerable. By incorporating mindfulness into daily life, individuals can develop greater self-awareness and self-acceptance, which can lead to greater happiness and well-being.

Overcoming self-criticism

Overcoming self-criticism is an important aspect of developing self-compassion through mindfulness. Self-criticism can lead to a negative self-image, low self-esteem, and increased stress levels. The following are techniques for overcoming self-criticism and cultivating self-compassion:

1. Mindful self-awareness: The first step in overcoming self-criticism is to become aware of the negative self-talk and inner critic. Pay attention to the thoughts and feelings that arise when you engage in self-criticism. Observe these thoughts and feelings with a non-judgmental attitude and try to understand where they come from.

2. Self-compassionate self-talk: Replace self-criticism with self-compassionate self-talk. When you notice negative self-talk, try to reframe it in a positive, self-compassionate way. For example, instead of saying "I'm so stupid for making that mistake," try saying "It's okay to make mistakes. I can learn from this and do better next time."

3. Practice self-forgiveness: Forgiving oneself is an important step in overcoming self-criticism. Instead of holding onto past mistakes and beating yourself up over them, practice self-forgiveness. Recognize that everyone makes mistakes and that you are worthy of self-compassion and forgiveness.

4. Focus on strengths: Instead of dwelling on weaknesses and mistakes, focus on your strengths and positive qualities. Mindfully acknowledge your strengths and cultivate a sense of self-appreciation.

5. Cultivate self-acceptance: Accept yourself as you are, flaws and all. Mindfully observe your thoughts and feelings without judgment or criticism. Embrace your imperfections and recognize that they are a natural part of being human.

6. Practice gratitude: Practicing gratitude can help shift your focus from self-criticism to self-compassion. Mindfully appreciate the good things in your life and express gratitude for them. This can help cultivate a sense of self-worth and self-compassion.

7. Seek support: It can be helpful to seek support from friends, family, or a mental health professional when struggling with self-criticism. Talking about your feelings and experiences can help you gain perspective and develop self-compassion.

Overall, overcoming self-criticism and developing self-compassion is a gradual process that requires patience and self-awareness. By practicing mindfulness and self-compassion, you can cultivate a more positive self-image and increase your overall well-being.

Cultivating a sense of gratitude and appreciation

Cultivating a sense of gratitude and appreciation is an important aspect of developing self-compassion through mindfulness practice. Gratitude involves recognizing and acknowledging the good things in one's life, while appreciation involves feeling grateful for those things and recognizing their value.

Research has shown that practicing gratitude can have a positive impact on mental health and well-being. A study published in the Journal of Personality and Social Psychology found that participants who kept a gratitude journal for ten weeks had better mental health outcomes than those who did not. Participants in the gratitude journal group reported feeling more optimistic, happier, and had fewer physical complaints compared to the control group.

Practicing gratitude can also have a positive impact on relationships. A study published in the journal Emotion found that expressing gratitude towards a partner can lead to increased feelings of love and connection.

Mindfulness practice can help individuals cultivate a sense of gratitude and appreciation by bringing their attention to the present moment and focusing on the positive aspects of their lives. This can involve taking time each day to reflect on what one is grateful for, such as good health, supportive relationships, or fulfilling work. Mindful breathing and body scan exercises can also be helpful in cultivating a sense of gratitude by helping individuals connect with their body and the present moment.

Another way to cultivate gratitude is to practice acts of kindness towards oneself and others. This can involve small acts of kindness such as offering a kind word to a colleague or taking time to care for one's physical and emotional needs. Mindfulness practice can help individuals become more aware of opportunities for kindness and appreciate the positive impact it has on their well-being and the well-being of others.

In addition to gratitude, cultivating a sense of appreciation can also be beneficial for developing self-compassion. Appreciation involves recognizing the value of one's experiences, accomplishments, and personal qualities. This can help individuals feel more confident and self-assured, which can lead to improved mental health outcomes.

Mindfulness practice can help individuals cultivate appreciation by bringing their attention to the present moment and recognizing the positive aspects of their experiences. This can involve taking time to reflect on one's accomplishments and personal qualities, such as resilience, creativity, or compassion. Mindfulness meditation can also be helpful in cultivating appreciation by allowing individuals to develop a deeper sense of connection with themselves and their experiences.

Overall, cultivating a sense of gratitude and appreciation is an important aspect of developing self-compassion through mindfulness practice. By focusing on the positive aspects of one's life and experiences, individuals can develop a greater sense of well-being and improve their relationships with themselves and others.

Conclusion
The benefits of mindfulness and meditation for mental and emotional well-being

Mindfulness and meditation have become increasingly popular in recent years as more people recognize their potential benefits for mental and emotional well-being. The practice of mindfulness involves paying attention to the present moment with openness and curiosity, while meditation involves intentionally focusing one's attention to achieve a state of calm and clarity. These practices have been shown to have a wide range of benefits, from reducing stress and anxiety to improving sleep and increasing overall well-being.

One of the key benefits of mindfulness and meditation is their ability to reduce stress and anxiety. When we practice mindfulness, we become more aware of our thoughts and emotions, allowing us to recognize and respond to stressors more effectively. Meditation can also help reduce the physical symptoms of stress, such as high blood pressure and muscle tension, by promoting relaxation and a sense of calm.

In addition to reducing stress, mindfulness and meditation can also improve our overall emotional well-being. Research has shown that these practices can help alleviate symptoms of depression and anxiety, improve mood, and increase feelings of happiness and well-being. They can also help us better regulate our emotions, allowing us to respond to difficult situations in a more balanced and effective way.

Mindfulness and meditation can also have a positive impact on our physical health. Studies have shown that these practices can lower blood pressure, improve immune function, and even reduce symptoms of chronic pain. In addition, meditation has been found to improve sleep quality, which can have a wide range of health benefits.

Another benefit of mindfulness and meditation is their ability to increase our capacity for compassion and empathy. By cultivating a sense of awareness and connection with others, we can become more attuned to their needs and better able to respond with kindness and compassion. This can help us build stronger relationships and feel more connected to our communities.

Finally, mindfulness and meditation can help us develop a deeper sense of self-awareness and self-acceptance. By paying attention to our thoughts and emotions without judgment, we can learn to accept ourselves more fully and cultivate a greater sense of self-compassion. This can lead to increased self-esteem and a more positive self-image.

In conclusion, the benefits of mindfulness and meditation for mental and emotional well-being are clear. By reducing stress and anxiety, improving emotional well-being, promoting physical health, increasing compassion and empathy, and fostering self-awareness and self-acceptance, these practices can have a profound impact on our lives. Whether we are seeking to improve our relationships, increase productivity, or simply feel better overall, mindfulness and meditation offer a powerful tool for personal growth and transformation.

Encouragement to continue practicing mindfulness and meditation

Mindfulness and meditation can have significant benefits for our mental and emotional well-being. They can help us manage stress, improve our relationships, increase our productivity, and develop self-compassion. However, it's important to remember that these benefits are not always immediate or obvious, and that mindfulness is a practice that requires consistent effort and dedication.

To encourage continued practice, it can be helpful to reflect on the benefits that have already been experienced. For example, one might think about how mindfulness has helped them manage a particularly stressful situation, or how it has improved their ability to communicate with others. These reflections can serve as motivation to continue practicing and exploring the benefits of mindfulness.

It's also important to remember that mindfulness can take many forms, and that there is no "right" way to practice. Some people may prefer guided meditations or body scans, while others may find mindfulness in movement practices like yoga or tai chi. Additionally, mindfulness can be practiced in any moment, even in the midst of daily tasks like washing dishes or walking the dog.

Another way to encourage continued practice is to find a community of others who are also interested in mindfulness and meditation. This might include attending a regular meditation group or class, joining an online community, or even just finding a friend or family member to practice with. Having support and accountability can be a powerful motivator for continuing to practice.

Finally, it's important to approach mindfulness and meditation with a sense of curiosity and openness. The practice is not about achieving a particular goal or outcome, but rather about cultivating awareness and presence in the present moment. This means letting go of expectations and judgments, and simply allowing the experience to unfold. By approaching mindfulness with an open mind and heart, we can continue to deepen our understanding and practice over time.

In conclusion, practicing mindfulness and meditation can have profound benefits for our mental and emotional well-being. Encouraging continued practice involves reflecting on the benefits already experienced, exploring different forms of practice, finding community support, and approaching the practice with openness and curiosity. By continuing to cultivate mindfulness and meditation in our daily lives, we can experience greater peace, happiness, and fulfillment.

Further resources for exploring mindfulness and meditation

In conclusion, mindfulness and meditation are powerful tools that can help individuals achieve greater mental and emotional well-being. The benefits of these practices are numerous, ranging from reduced stress and anxiety to increased focus and productivity. By incorporating mindfulness and meditation into our daily lives, we can develop greater self-awareness and cultivate a sense of inner peace and contentment.

For those interested in exploring mindfulness and meditation further, there are many resources available. One option is to seek out local meditation groups or mindfulness classes in your community. Many yoga studios and wellness centers offer classes on a regular basis. Another option is to explore online resources, such as guided meditations and mindfulness apps. These resources can provide a convenient and accessible way to practice mindfulness and meditation from the comfort of your own home.

Additionally, there are many books and articles available that delve into the practice of mindfulness and meditation in greater depth. Some popular titles include "Mindfulness in Plain English" by Bhante Gunaratana, "The Power of Now" by Eckhart Tolle, and "10% Happier" by Dan

Harris. These resources can provide a deeper understanding of the benefits of mindfulness and meditation and offer guidance on how to incorporate these practices into daily life.

Finally, it is important to remember that mindfulness and meditation are not quick-fix solutions. Developing a consistent practice takes time and patience, and progress may be slow at times. However, the benefits of mindfulness and meditation are well worth the effort. By continuing to practice and explore these techniques, individuals can achieve greater peace of mind, improved emotional well-being, and a more fulfilling life.

THE END

Wordbook

Welcome to the glossary section of this book. Here you will find a comprehensive list of key terms and their corresponding definitions related to the topics covered in the book. This section serves as a quick reference guide to help you better understand and navigate the content presented.

1. Mindfulness: A mental state characterized by awareness and attention to the present moment, without judgment or distraction.

2. Meditation: A technique for cultivating mindfulness and other positive mental states, often involving focused attention, deep breathing, and visualization.

3. Stress reduction: The process of reducing the physiological and psychological effects of stress on the body and mind.

4. Emotional regulation: The ability to manage and control one's own emotions, particularly in response to stressful or challenging situations.

5. Self-compassion: The practice of treating oneself with kindness, understanding, and nonjudgment, particularly in times of difficulty or suffering.

6. Empathy: The ability to understand and share the feelings of another person.

7. Compassion: The desire to alleviate the suffering of others, often characterized by kindness, generosity, and empathy.

8. Productivity: The ability to efficiently and effectively complete tasks and achieve goals.

9. Gratitude: The feeling of being thankful and appreciative for the positive aspects of one's life, even in the face of difficulty or challenge.

10. Resilience: The ability to recover quickly from setbacks or adversity, often through the cultivation of positive mental states like mindfulness and self-compassion.

Supplementary Materials

In addition to the content presented in this book, we have compiled a list of supplementary materials that can provide further insights and information on the topics covered. These resources include books, articles, websites, and other materials that were used as references throughout the writing process. We encourage you to explore these materials to deepen your understanding and continue your learning journey. Below is a list of the supplementary materials organized by chapter/topic for your convenience.

Introduction

Kabat-Zinn, J. (1994). Wherever you go, there you are: Mindfulness meditation in everyday life. Hyperion.

Chapter 1: Mindfulness

Brown, K. W., & Ryan, R. M. (2003). The benefits of being present: Mindfulness and its role in psychological well-being. Journal of Personality and Social Psychology, 84(4), 822-848.

Chapter 2: Meditation

Lutz, A., Slagter, H. A., Dunne, J. D., & Davidson, R. J. (2008). Attention regulation and monitoring in meditation. Trends in Cognitive Sciences, 12(4), 163-169.

Chapter 3: Establishing a Meditation Practice

Salzberg, S. (2011). Real happiness: The power of meditation. Workman Publishing.

Chapter 4: Mindfulness-Based Stress Reduction

Kabat-Zinn, J. (1990). Full catastrophe living: Using the wisdom of your body and mind to face stress, pain, and illness. Dell Publishing.

Chapter 5: Mindfulness and Relationships

Carson, J. W., Carson, K. M., Gil, K. M., & Baucom, D. H. (2004). Mindfulness-based relationship enhancement. Behavior Therapy, 35(3), 471-494.

Chapter 6: Mindfulness and Productivity

Dane, E. (2011). Paying attention to mindfulness and its effects on task performance in the workplace. Journal of Management, 37(4), 997-1018.

Chapter 7: Mindfulness and Self-Compassion

Neff, K. (2011). Self-compassion: The proven power of being kind to yourself. HarperCollins.

Conclusion

Baer, R. A. (2015). Mindfulness-based treatment approaches: Clinician's guide to evidence base and applications. Academic Press.

www.ingramcontent.com/pod-product-compliance
Lightning Source LLC
LaVergne TN
LVHW010400070526
838199LV00065B/5867